Terms and Conditions

LEGAL NOTICE

The Publisher has strived to be as accurate and complete as possible in the creation of this report, notwithstanding the fact that he does not warrant or represent at any time that the contents within are accurate due to the rapidly changing nature of the Internet.

While all attempts have been made to verify information provided in this publication, the Publisher assumes no responsibility for errors, omissions, or contrary interpretation of the subject matter herein. Any perceived slights of specific persons, peoples, or organizations are unintentional.

In practical advice books, like anything else in life, there are no guarantees of income made. Readers are cautioned to reply on their own judgment about their individual circumstances to act accordingly.

This book is not intended for use as a source of legal, business, accounting or financial advice. All readers are advised to seek services of competent professionals in legal, business, accounting and finance fields.

You are encouraged to print this book for easy reading.

Table Of Contents

Foreword

Chapter 1:
How Important Is Customer Loyalty

Chapter 2:
Discern Where You Are In Respect To CustomerLoyalty

Chapter 3:
Understand Your Target Audience And TheirNeeds

Chapter 4:
Supply Products Of Worth To Fulfill A Need

Chapter 5:
Make Sure Your Customer Service Is Exceptional

Chapter 6:
Everyone In The Organization Must Be Trained ToReflect Your Vision

Wrapping Up

Foreword

Customer loyalty is the single most important element to retain within a business relationship. A lot of positive elements can be derived from a well established loyal customer base. Huge amounts of money is periodically allocated to advertising, primarily to garner a bigger market share of consumers, but with the existence of a loyal customer base, this expenses can be channeled towards other better and more beneficial areas.

Customer Retention Force

How To Develop Unstoppable Loyalty From Your Customer Base

Chapter 1:

How Important Is Customer Loyalty

Synopsis

Companies which have a satisfactory percentage of loyal customers have the advantage of channeling funds into a self reinforcing system in which the company delivers constantly evolving superior value and high quality products and services.

This will further create the comfortable relationship desired to continue to successfully keep the customers both happy and loyal.

There is also the added advantage of the preexisting customers who consciously help to introduce friends and family to consider using the products and services based on personal testimonies and enthusiasm.

The Basics

Another importance of retaining loyal customer ratios at an all time high lies in the fact that companies are able to focus on providing good customer induction schemes that contribute to a higher yielding customer base and thus provide for higher profits by reducing the need to spend money attracting potential but not necessarily viable customers. However such schemes should in no way take the place of good and resoundingly exemplary customer service.

The element of trust is rather hard to accomplish and even harder to nurture, but with the right daily process in place and use without deviation it is very possible to build the desired trust factor between both parties.

This trust factor will then translate to converting the casual customer into a loyal one. Thus any complains or misgivings regarding the products or services should be addressed swiftly and to the satisfaction of the customer. Companies that take the grievances of a customer seriously are usually the ones that have the highest loyal customer base on record.

Chapter 2:

Discern Where You Are In Respect To Customer Loyalty

Synopsis

Being able to discern one's position with regards to the customer loyalty ratio can be rather tricky if not virtually impossible sometimes. However thankfully there are some tried and true methods that can be used to achieve this goal.

Get It Figured Out

Being able to retain a loyal customer base has its merits and understanding the customer sentiment is pivotal to achieving this loyalty factor.

As loyal customers are a good indicator to a thriving and consistently successful business endeavor, taking the time to focus on understanding the level of each customer's loyalty is both prudent and beneficial in the long term state.

This understanding can help predict to a certain extent the ratio between the potentially loyal customer and those who may not ever become the desired loyal customer needed to keep the business a success.

By making this discovery the company can then take the necessary action to try to prevent potential customers from just being one time users.

Some things to seriously consider in the quest to understand the company's position within the customer's mindset would be as follows:

• Making the effort to gather the required data to assess the potential customer's reason for making the purchase or for showing an interest in the service or product offered.

• Finding out if the customer would be willing or even happy to introduce the product or service to others.

• Getting feedback of the level of satisfaction derived from using the product or the lack of said satisfaction. Armed with this information, there should also be a proactive counter action to address any negative feedback learnt.

• With the information gained from the customers, there should be a concerted effort to make the necessary improvements to the products or services to further encourage the commitment on the part of the customer to stay loyal.

Chapter 3:
Understand Your Target Audience And Their Needs

Synopsis

To a certain extent perceptions are made based on the knowledge garnered through specific means. However these means and methods may not always be reliable thus creating the possibility of ineffective handling of any problems or needs that may arise. For any product or service to become a success and sustain itself there is a definite advantage to understanding the target audience and their needs.

What's Needed

The importance of understanding this process is to effectively eliminate any wastage of effort and resources on wrong perceptions made. Understanding the difference between the actual needs of the target audience and measuring it against the perceived needs that the seller has been given to understand will help the seller to redefine the product or service to focus on the afore mentioned fact.

Sometimes however such information can be rather difficult to process as the customer themselves may not entirely know what they specifically need or want. This can be looked upon as an advantage on the part of the seller as it creates the opportunity for the seller to promote the product or service in a way that is attractive to the customer.

Also when the customer's needs are clearly understood, there can then be a clearer method used to garner the interest and possible successful sale. Advertising and information can be specifically designed to attract the customer based on the information learnt.

Continuously adapting to the customer's interests will allow for the success rates to be better in ensuring the loyalty factor. This in itself can contribute further in creating the customer's faith in the product or service being offered; as it portrays the commitment levels the company is willing to take to ensure the customer stays happy.

All these points are designed to address the customer's needs and interests.

Chapter 4:
Supply Products Of Worth To Fulfill A Need

Synopsis

The key to identifying and creating products that are likely to be well received by potential customers lie within the successful understanding of the needs both on the conscious and subconscious levels. As most people are unaware of what their needs and wants really are, the best designed advertising tools can be used to trigger the desire for a particular product or service.

Supply

As potential business entities, it is the primary function to accurately identify and nurture such needs in the potential customer. Taking the time and effort to research products that are worth the customer's attention will eventually garner the desired results of encouraging purchases.

It would be prudent to never underestimate or disregard any customer sentiments as this will eventually cause the customer to look elsewhere for their needs.

Once the relevant data is gathered, the company should focus on searching and presenting products that would be viable and interesting to the potential customer base.

When such products are identified as suitable according to the research done, the customer should then be effectively encouraged to make the effort to commit to purchasing the said product.

These product should at all times be of a certain high quality as this important factor is often the deciding point on the customer's behalf between staying loyal and buying randomly.

Another important consideration should be to constantly provide the customer with updated and better versions of the product or service as in keeping with the current times and requirements that may arise.

Innovatively evolving product are usually well received and eventually anticipated. Besides feeling valued on the part of the customer because of the willingness of the company to provide new products often, the customer will also be happier to introduce the said items to others.

Chapter 5:
Make Sure Your Customer Service Is Exceptional

Synopsis

Most businesses today offer very similar products or services, thus the few ways and individual can ensure an edge over his or her competitors is to strive to provide exceptional customer service.

Customer Care

Product today don't really vary too much in terms of functions and price ranges, thus by taking the trouble to provide good customer services the potential customer can be persuaded to consider making repeat purchases.

Below are just some recommendations one can follow in the quest to provide exceptional customer services:

• As most initial enquiries are done over the phone, making it a habit to return or respond to all phone communications is very important and definitely advisable. Doing so in a prompt manner is also another way of making the customer feel important.

• Providing a follow up service or enquiry into the satisfaction of the product or service help both parties gain vital information and builds a relationship of trust and commitment. This also allows the individual an insight to the expectations of the customer.

• Being committed enough to go the extra "mile" is another very important and positive feature in practice. Customers are often put off by this clearly diminishing quality and when extended, the customer will definitely be adequately impressed.

- Taking the customer's concerns seriously and implementing the necessary steps to address these concerns is also another beneficial trait of exceptional customer service. This not only relieves the customers concerns but also establishes the company's commitment to the customer satisfaction guarantee.

- Though sometimes very difficult indeed, there is a very important need to stay focused and view the problem from the customer's perspective. When confronted with a problem a customer can more often than not make unrealistic claims and remarks, thus having a calm demeanor would help to defuse any potentially unpleasant situation.

Chapter 6:
Everyone In The Organization Must Be Trained To Reflect Your Vision

Synopsis

To work effectively and for one common goal within the company it is very important for all involved to share the same vision. This vision should be clearly defined so that all involved understand the direction in which the company envisions for its product or service, as this makes it easier for all to reach the clearly defined goals reflected through the unified vision.

Possibilities

Having a leadership role or any role within the workings of the company where the vision is clearly outlined and accepted allows for the creation of a set of successful and effective action plan, belief system, values and goals ratio.

Having a clearly defined and powerful vision for the company and ensuring it is completely followed and reflected by all, helps to encourage everyone to incorporate the said vision into their everyday work life to produce the desired positive results.

These visions should be well thought out and appealing to further cultivate the feeling of comradeship and oneness in belonging to something bigger and better than one's own self. It is also what helps to drive everyone to reach their best potential achievements because of the excitement it generates.

When visions are clearly defined by the organization's direction and purpose it should help to inspire loyalty and caring attitudes, which will be displayed and reflected in the unique strengths, that brings about the positive attributes of enthusiasm, belief and commitment of the excited employees.

Wrapping Up

Visions for the company can help each individual to challenge themselves to reach higher and previously unthought-of goals. Through the formation of appropriate visions for the company it is also hoped that those involved will feel a sense of importance and appreciation and thus continue to strive to do their best both for the company and for themselves.

www.ingramcontent.com/pod-product-compliance
Lightning Source LLC
Chambersburg PA
CBHW031511210526
45463CB00008B/3196